The Rhythm Of Poetry

Zaire Hodges

The Rhythm of Poetry
By: Zaire Hodges

Cover created and designed by: Jazzy Kitty Publishing
Logo designs by: Andre M. Saunders and Leroy Grayson
Editor: Jazzy Kitty Publishing

© 2012 Zaire Hodges

ISBN: 978-0-9830548-7-0
Library of Congress Control Number: 2011963235

All rights reserved. This book is protected under the copyright laws of the United States of America. This book may not be copied or reprinted for commercial gain or profit. The use of short quotations or occasional page copying for personal or group study is permitted and encouraged. Permission will be granted upon request.

For Worldwide Distribution. Printed in the United States of America. Published by Jazzy Kitty Greetings Marketing & Publishing, LLC dba Jazzy Kitty Publishing. Utilizing Microsoft Publishing Software.

EPILOGUE

I hope I have made an inerasable mind print. That you will take with you on your journey through life. The main reason I wrote the novel is to inspire, but also to set a braking of the cycle of only white gay and lesbian novel writers. In all the history of the gay and lesbian fiction writings, there were only white characters and few books on females dealing with this issue. And the atomic reason finally is that there was no recording of an African American Author or diverse characters in this area of writing.

My novel happens to have diversity in the characters; Rain is Asian and half-black. Nubia is black and Cameron is a light-brown black. Nia is bi-racial, Bayar is Chinese, and Felicia is light skinned. But no matter their color they have one common goal, which is to be accepted as people. With this novel, I am glad to be the first African American Author of a fiction book like this one.

And also to be the first person to have a novel with many different diversities.

In closing, it is an honor to create change for many.

ACKNOWLEDGMENTS

I want to thank everyone who helped make this novel a reality.

I also want to thank everyone who helped with the creation of the cover.

I want to thank everyone's contributions to the novel itself also the publishing company.

I want to thank my wonderful fantastic imagination.

This book is for everyone who's felt different and is powerful & amazing-beyond normal expectations.
- *(Zaire Hodges)*

I am a human being nothing human can be alien to me.
- *By Terence*

I want to thank my first-grade teacher; she formed my love of writing, thank you.

You must have a fantasy to have reality.
- *Quote Jimmy Hendrix's*

DEDICATIONS

This book is dedicated to everyone who has helped mold me into the brilliant beautiful young women I am.

To my mom and dad for letting me be free with my craft of writing and respecting what I choose to write about that will matter.

To my loving family, I thank all of you.

Also to my close friends who inspired me.

To Almighty to God for giving me this great gift and blessing me a million times and counting.

And to Kim who is my muse for my writing and has brought happiness and love and for everything and much more to my life.

Inspirational quote: Everything is a gift. The longest journey begins with a single step.

One of my greatest lessons I had learned from my Great Granny, she told me when I was elementary school age when I was with her. She told me you're going to do something really special. I believed her. Now I know what that is to write about things people don't want to talk about and help heal the world with my words. Thank you, I love you. And miss you.

TABLE OF CONTENTS

Introduction i
Love Poem 01
Understanding the Rhythm of Poetry 03
Stereotypes that Need to be Addressed 05
Felicia's Truth Essay 07
Identity 11
The Meeting 12
Wake Up 19
Apartment Love 21
Success for Bayar 23
New Life 25
Spending Time 27
Insult to Leave 30
Labor of Love 32
Felicia Gets Her Book Published 33
Christmas Gathering... This is Family 35
About the Author 37

INTRODUCTION

In the book Felicia and her friends take a life journey together to eliminate the question of what is normal? As they enter life with loves and ponders the tedious amazing question of: What is a family?

Is there a common goal to find out what many have tried to say does not exist or could never find out that there is no such thing as a perfect person or perfect creation of a loving family.

TABLE OF CONTENTS

Introduction i
Love Poem 01
Understanding the Rhythm of Poetry 03
Stereotypes that Need to be Addressed 05
Felicia's Truth Essay 07
Identity 11
The Meeting 12
Wake Up 19
Apartment Love 21
Success for Bayar 23
New Life 25
Spending Time 27
Insult to Leave 30
Labor of Love 32
Felicia Gets Her Book Published 33
Christmas Gathering... This is Family 35
About the Author 37

INTRODUCTION

In the book Felicia and her friends take a life journey together to eliminate the question of what is normal? As they enter life with loves and ponders the tedious amazing question of: What is a family?

Is there a common goal to find out what many have tried to say does not exist or could never find out that there is no such thing as a perfect person or perfect creation of a loving family.

The Rhythm of Poetry

Zaire Hodges

LOVE POEM...
Audre Lorde

I think she was excited to publish the poem in her book tilted *The Land Where Other People Live;* she gave it to another poet to read. He was a man and also a poet; he said, "Now what is this, are you supposed to be a man?" She replied back to the insulting comment, "No; I am a loving woman." She also said, "He did not publish *Love Poem* the first time around; and then he did, but I took it out." Audre replied when asked why by an interviewer and a friend. "Why did she take it out?" "I am guessing she was at a poetry sharing; she had read it." she replied. Then she said, "I read it with myself at the back of the wall by then after reading it, I had made up my mind that I did not worry who knows and who did not know." Referring to her lesbianism and the lesbian poem. Then she said she took it out. I am guessing she got scared again and had decided not to put it in the book which I thought was okay because we all are a little scared sometimes, so I completely understand as a writer. So Audre too published but also let alone read a lesbian poem is scary. I don't think she contradicted herself although other people might not understand. You can read *Love Poem* on the internet after it being found in Audrey's collection of poems and journals. They had found that poem. A lot of her journals are at museums in New York. Including something I had not known that they had a lesbian museum. Some of her journals are at The Lesbian Museum in Brooklyn New York. When I had read *Love Poem*, I felt amazed by the details and metaphors of love she had used in the poem.

(Felicia)

The Rhythm of Poetry

Zaire Hodges

UNDERSTANDING THE RHYTHM OF POETRY AND THE MEANING OF WORDS

I have to say I had formed my love of poetry in seventh grade, as soon as I finally clearly understood it. For a long time, I had just thought and had viewed it as a person going up to the microphone and just saying words. As time when on I got rid of that idea. Then came the mixed messages of some poems I got and others I didn't. And the ones I did not understand or know what was going on. I try endlessly to search for the meaning or over all the point in what it is about. And almost every time I fail and be utterly defeated by those poems, so I began to read easy poems the work up to the hard ones then finally I got it. And had decided to write a poem just one to see if I could. I realized I was a natural poet and feel in love with poetry. And read every one that interested me from Langston Hugh's to Melvin B. Tolson, Audre Lorde, and other poets.

I have written six poems so far. As a writer I go back and explore the words I thought were bad; words in First grade. When I began to write and spell words, the words I thought were bad ones. Not only, in writing but in speaking period. Like

The Rhythm of Poetry
Zaire Hodges

the words shut up and mammy. Later, I found out, *"mammy"* means maid. I though all that time I prohibited myself from ever saying it out of my mouth. That it was a rude slave term not to be used.

I know one word was never to be used in specking or writing. The "N" word I was never going to say it. But I just wanted to know the meaning of it. Someone told me, they had said the "N" word, and it was a word that describes a person who is not classy or flat out ignorant no-good person. That was everything rude, nasty, and no respect. I was in shock after they had finished, and I said, "Thank you for telling me what that means." I did not say much after that; it took me a week to get over the meaning of the "N" word.

When other kids in my class later in Fifth grade were looking up at that time the nasty word *sex* in the dictionary, and I thought it was gross.

(By Felicia/really Zaire's words & thoughts on this page.)

STEREOTYPES THAT NEED TO BE ADDRESSED

In many ways, a lot of people as fashion designers and lesbian writers have tried to diminish this stereotype of lesbians including the ones placed in are cultures, like the Black community. That there's only one form of lesbianism, the *boyish* kind; the Black female lesbian who looks so much like a guy, and it's very hard to tell if she's a boy or a girl. That's the only one they see, they can't know about the *girlish* full-fledged lesbian woman. The ones who are *still* girls but are just lesbian. They never see her; also, they have alienated us from a normal female talking and gossiping. They think normal female behaviors are awkward when they see us like shopping, and having fun with non-gay friends. Saying you can't have fun with other females as a friend. They say statements like, *"I thought you were gay?"* They have also forgotten that the boyish lesbian is a girl too, and they do have female friends but dresses a little differently. The most aggravating statements are the ones like we're *still not* girls is, *"Why are you buying a purse, gay girls don't do that?"*

The most logical reason given in the dumbest annoying

context is, "Why are you getting your hair done? Gay girls don't do that?" they asked. I guess they think we're supposed to all have page boys and not look as beautiful as other women with long flowing hair; and not have hair flowing in the air like an Ebony Magazine model. Also, the clothing dilemma is rude.

Everyone thinks that gay girls should not wear skirts, earrings, hair clips, gardenias, or bracelets; and should all wear pants, and a male or lesbian stereotype tops. And have not a stitch of feminism or the idea we're girls and women just like your type of vibe.

In closing this essay, the stereotypes over clothing needs to stop.

(Essay by Felicia)

The Rhythm of Poetry

Zaire Hodges

FELICIA'S TRUTH ESSAY

Felicia's Truth Essay May 3, 2011 Me Felecia's truth is real big. Let me Felicia, start off with how I look. I got really long flowing black hair to my shoulders. I am light skin; I have black eyes, and I am kind of gothic, but I don't wear black all the time. Like right now, I am wearing a black-and-white striped long- sleeve shirt and dark black pants with chains on the side pockets. Like the ones at the gothic store, *HOT TOPIC* and I carry a *Hello Kitty* bag; it's all black with *Hello Kitty* on the front.

I love Audre Lorde poems. And I live in New York right next to Time Square. I live one block away; I can just walk there. I am in high school; I am seventeen, and I am home schooled because I had problems at my old school; it shutdown because of the inability to pay. My Home School teacher name is Mr. Brinkley; he's cool, and he teaches me everything I need to know.

He knows about my old girlfriend & Bayar, my long one. I moved out last month to my own apartment. Not that far from my parents but a good little while away. I live on the fifth floor.

The Rhythm of Poetry
Zaire Hodges

In it, there are four rooms with lots of space. I pay rent by working at a pharmacy Monday through Wednesday, then Thursday and Friday, I have days off. My work partner is Owen; he constantly reads stuff when we're supposed to be doing work. He's reading Twilight or on the internet on T.M.Z. He restocks the shelves of idioms; he's always in the food area or elsewhere.

Annoyingly every other day he had asked me, "When are you going to stop being Goth?" I said, "I don't think ever." He said looking in a magazine, "Did you know all these women in this are fake?" he said. I said with a slow shrug, "Yes Owen, I know."

I side tracked and put in Lady GaGa's Born This Way Album; I turn it up. Lady Gaga says it doesn't matter if you love him or capital H.I.M. just put your paws up. When the song started Owen said, "Why do you like her anyway?" I said, "Because... she's great!" He said, "Well this song definitely goes to your demo graphic of..." I stopped him in mid sentence with a look. He said, "Feel, I am sorry." *(My nickname he calls me)*. Then he changed the subject.

"Hey I got you another Audre Lorde book from Borders. It's

The Rhythm of Poetry
Zaire Hodges

called Warrior Poet." he said. "Thanks." I replied. "You're welcome." he said back.

He went to the closet in the store and got the book. I put it in my *Hello Kitty* bag. Then I told Owen I am having a party at my apartment.

He asked, "When?" I said, "Back Friday night." "Kool, I will be there." he said. Then added, "You think I can score any hot chicks?" "I don't know." I said back.

Here's what Owen looks like; he has short and curly at the top of his head black hair, an employee T-shirt and jeans. He's white and wears thick glasses. And always tries to imitate singers.

Owen asked, "How's Bayar and how did you two meet?" I said, "We met at a meeting in two thousand and three." Then he wanted to know the whole thing. He also said, "That's why you dumped the other one before Bayar?" "Yes." I said. "Bayar's better for you." Owen said relaxing.

When I got to Target, I grabbed a cart, and started putting things in it. Like party napkins, plates, bowls, Kool Aid, Ginger ale, Pepsi, and Orange Crush. Then the snacks Ritz Crackers, Chips Ahoy, Oreos, Tostitos Tortilla Chips, cheese sauce, Wheat

The Rhythm of Poetry

Zaire Hodges

Thins, Cheese Doodles, and marshmallows. That's all I needed, my friend worked for a catering company who does soul food dishes was catering the party. Also she and the rest of the workers were coming by with the food for the party with ham, turkey, fried fish, deviled eggs, red rice, yellow rice, mash potatoes, sweet potatoes, fried chicken, collard greens, corn bread, fried salmon, macaroni and cheese, fried okra, black-eyed peas soup, and individual pecan pies. I was already preparing to make a big pan of Rice Krispies Treats in a baking pan. Josephine had told me Mrs. Mable the co-owner of SOUTHERN DELICASES was helping her bring the food since Mrs. Rita Washington was making biscuits for a dinner party. Twenty-seven of them and a big old pot of black-eyed peas soup. And twenty-eight corn bread orders. Josephine and Mrs. Mable cooked all the food for my gathering the day before in the big kitchen.

I went home with Chinese chicken, ate it, and watched *He's Just Not into You,* with a bowl of popcorn in my hands. Then I heard a knock at my door; it was Owen. He came in and watched it with me. Tomorrow was my day off, and I was definitely going to spend it.

The Rhythm of Poetry

Zaire Hodges

IDENTITY

Poem by Felicia

My identity outline was a reflection of me...

My goal was to be lesbian and free...

Not left in the cold dark shadows of the...

Muted insides of me free so that birds...

Can sing forever in peace without being...

Disturbed with social grief free with the wind...

In my long flowing hair and my rainbow dress...

No longer could country or personal mess...

Free to love with open arms and to work my mythical...

Human charm announced to me as a student, lesbian, or human.

(Felicia's poem about herself)

THE MEETING
3/12/2003

I must say I have never been to a gay & lesbian meeting, but Mr. Brinkley dragged me to one today; he was like you need to go and confront what you are. And he said, "Get out of that chair referring to the chair I was planted in. I am taking you somewhere." As we drove in the taxi, I questioned where was I going? In my head, then we were there at the gay & lesbian building, we got out the taxi.

Mr. Brinkley walked faster than I in there. I was lagging behind because I was scared. I had on a plain long sleeve green shirt, a black skirt, and fashion boots. I walked in behind Mr. Brinkley the lady at the front desk asked my name. I am too weak to answer her; I am glad that I am here but nervous. Mr. Brinkley said my name. "Her name is Felicia." he said. He also asked, "Where is the meeting?" The lady said, "Right down the hall on your left." We passed the white wall into a big orange room with chairs in a circle. I crossed over all the other teens there and found a seat. I sit in the light blue plastic chair theirs different color plastic chairs; there's a green one, orange one,

The Rhythm of Poetry
Zaire Hodges

yellow one, purple one, and pink one.

The mentor and teacher came in, his name is Fernando. He said, "I am Fernando." He seemed nice so far. Mr. Brinkley sitting in the back with all the other people that brought everyone in the circle to the meeting. Fernando said, "Let's start okay." We go around telling each other's name.

One guys name was Cameron, he's funny. He said, "My name is Cameron, hey." And we all laughed and he laughed too.

Then there's this other guy named Numbi; he said that his name comes from a foreign county, he also said that his mother visited while she was pregnant with him out of the states. Everybody liked his name in the circle.

The next person to go was a girl name Rain; she was pretty, light skinned, and got long hair too; but in one big braid. Numbi is black brown and Cameron light brown. Rain said her name and we asked her where was she from. She also said that she was half Asian, that explains her long good hair. She goes on to say; her dad is Asian and her mom is a light skinned black from New York. She learned how to speak Asian in collage, and that's how her mom and dad got together.

The Rhythm of Poetry
Zaire Hodges

Then it was my turn, I feel okay now. My name Felicia, I live alone in my own apartment after I moved out a year ago. I am home schooled by my teacher Mr. Brinkley; he stood up. Then I said, "He brought me here." Then he said, "I needed to say what I am." Then they clapped for me and I felt warm inside like they liked me. I sat back down.

Then the next person to go was another girl, she said, "My name is Bayar. I am Chinese, and I live in New York, down town in Time Square." I thought, that's where I live. She continues to say, "I live in Time Square with my two mothers, a Chinese one and a light skinned black one. I was conceived by I.V.F." Her light skinned mother could not conceive. Her Chinese mother made a baby with a black man's sperm and gave birth to their baby. She said, "I am half black and Chinese."

Bayar explained to us that she comes here because she is lesbian and her parents told her to go to talk with other people like herself. She said she feels good coming to talk. "I do too now." I said chiming in. Bayar finished by saying, "I have been coming for two weeks so far, and it has helped."

I took Bayar's advice; I put my name in the group on the sheet

The Rhythm of Poetry
Zaire Hodges

of what group you're in. The lady at the front desk name I finally know (with her name up there now), her name is Miss Mara, and she was nice. She said, "Thank you." We all waved bye to each other, and said we will see each other at the next meeting.

Then Bayar gets in the cab with me and Mr. Brinkley; she tells me that she lives on the same block as I do. We are both happy about that, I like her, but I don't tell her. We get off were we both live, walked, and hugged each other good bye. I enjoyed her hug, it felt like a sweet marshmallow. I can have fun with Bayar now because I left the other one because she lied.

Anyway, Bayar hugs me and then we leave each other; then I go in my apartment. Bayar is seventeen too. I heard a knock at the door; it's Bayar. She said she wants me to meet her parents. I go over to Bayar; she is wearing a dark-blue T-shirt with a red flower in the middle of the shirt, jeans, and Nikes with black around them with the Nike symbol in light pink. She takes me over three doors down, when we get to the fourth door, it's hers. She opened the door, and a tall light skinned women answered. Bayar said, "Mom this is Felicia." I stand up and

The Rhythm of Poetry

Zaire Hodges

Bayar said, "Felicia this is Millie, my mother." She said hello and I said hello back. Then Bayar took me more into the apartment. It's nice; it has tan pretty walls and elements of both home lands China and Africa. She introduced me to her other mother Kilan; she is Chinese. Then she leaves and said she going to my place, and I said bye. She gets in my apartment and goes crazy; she starts hugging and kissing me. And then before I knew it, Bayar and I (Felicia) were making out on my couch.

Bayar got long jet-black hair to her shoulders as well. She gave me her number after and said to call her in two days later, and I do. Also Mr. Brinkley told me to transfer to a gay and lesbian high school, so I don't feel alone. He's not my teacher any more but we're still friends.

I go take a tour of the school, and I fall in love with it. Numbi and Cameron go to my new school. Our teacher lets us read books on people like us, and write about how we feel with who we are. I go to p.s. 149 they're very nice too.

Party Crazy Thursday night I called Owen. He said he was in charge of preparing the snack bowls because the last party I accidentally put them in the wrong places; so I agreed to that.

Then I called Bayar, and we talked. I told her I was throwing

The Rhythm of Poetry
Zaire Hodges

of what group you're in. The lady at the front desk name I finally know (with her name up there now), her name is Miss Mara, and she was nice. She said, "Thank you." We all waved bye to each other, and said we will see each other at the next meeting.

Then Bayar gets in the cab with me and Mr. Brinkley; she tells me that she lives on the same block as I do. We are both happy about that, I like her, but I don't tell her. We get off were we both live, walked, and hugged each other good bye. I enjoyed her hug, it felt like a sweet marshmallow. I can have fun with Bayar now because I left the other one because she lied.

Anyway, Bayar hugs me and then we leave each other; then I go in my apartment. Bayar is seventeen too. I heard a knock at the door; it's Bayar. She said she wants me to meet her parents. I go over to Bayar; she is wearing a dark-blue T-shirt with a red flower in the middle of the shirt, jeans, and Nikes with black around them with the Nike symbol in light pink. She takes me over three doors down, when we get to the fourth door, it's hers. She opened the door, and a tall light skinned women answered. Bayar said, "Mom this is Felicia." I stand up and

The Rhythm of Poetry
Zaire Hodges

Bayar said, "Felicia this is Millie, my mother." She said hello and I said hello back. Then Bayar took me more into the apartment. It's nice; it has tan pretty walls and elements of both home lands China and Africa. She introduced me to her other mother Kilan; she is Chinese. Then she leaves and said she going to my place, and I said bye. She gets in my apartment and goes crazy; she starts hugging and kissing me. And then before I knew it, Bayar and I (Felicia) were making out on my couch.

Bayar got long jet-black hair to her shoulders as well. She gave me her number after and said to call her in two days later, and I do. Also Mr. Brinkley told me to transfer to a gay and lesbian high school, so I don't feel alone. He's not my teacher any more but we're still friends.

I go take a tour of the school, and I fall in love with it. Numbi and Cameron go to my new school. Our teacher lets us read books on people like us, and write about how we feel with who we are. I go to p.s. 149 they're very nice too.

Party Crazy Thursday night I called Owen. He said he was in charge of preparing the snack bowls because the last party I accidentally put them in the wrong places; so I agreed to that.

Then I called Bayar, and we talked. I told her I was throwing

The Rhythm of Poetry
Zaire Hodges

a big party at my apartment and she said she would come. Before I know it was Friday night. Owen showed up first and set up all the snacks. Josephine and Mrs. Mable was also there to help set up the food, and then Mrs. Mable left to see her daughter's five month-old baby. Josephine was staying to have fun. Then later everyone else came.

My friends from Fourth Studio Poetry Company where we hung out, all twenty of us every Thursday. I know my apartment was big. Then Cameron and Numbi showed up; Numbi came wearing a green T-shirt and black pants. It looked good next to his light hot chocolate completion.

Then Rain came in a purple dress, a black skinny purse with a gold chain on it; her necklace was also gold, and she had high pumps on. She brought her love Nia as well.

Nia had a red dress on and her long black hair was straitened. She was bi-racial and wore heels.

Then finally Bayar had come in with a green stretch dress. All the girls wore a stretch dress; Rain, Nia, Bayar, and I. As I was saying, Bayar had on a green stretch dress, a black bag, and boots high up to her knees; also her hair in a pony tail. Then I came with a light-blue stretch dress and straitened hair as well.

We danced and then ate Southern Delicacies food. Then the slow dances came on, and we all danced; Rain & Nia, Bayar & I. Cameron found a girl for this occasion and so did Numbi. And we had a fun time.

Bayar stayed over at my apartment after everyone cleaned up and left. She was with me on my Karlstad leather sofa. I said I was going to bed, I told Bayar she could sleep on the sofa.

The Rhythm of Poetry

Zaire Hodges

WAKE UP

3/15/2003

I had woken up at 9:16 am. Bayar was still asleep on my light cream colored sheets, and a soft pillow upon her head. Her long jet-black hair which she took out of a pony tail after the party, it was fully out and had a connection with the pillow. It draped almost past the pillow.

I was up already looking out my tall windows that had a ledge in the spaces of the walls; the rest of both walls were window.

Then Bayar began to wake up. I Felicia still could not believe I had let another human being in my apartment sleeping on my sofa. She was wearing a peach-colored night gown and had brought an extra change of clothing.

Bayar was awake sitting upright with her feet planted on the floor. She was rubbing her eyes and walked to the bathroom which was light pink and had an old claw-foot tub. It was already there before I moved in. She brushed her hair, came out walking forward towards me, and hugged me.

Then Bayar and I got dressed. She has on a green T- shirt, a

The Rhythm of Poetry
Zaire Hodges

black skirt with zippers, and heels. I had on a blue dress with white stripes and straitened hair. Bayar has her hair in one braid. We walked out of the apartment together arm and arm. We walked down town to get bagels; we ordered two English Muffins with butter and hot chocolate, we ate and then left. Then we went around town. We even went to the Lesbian Museum in Brooklyn were Audre Lorde's journals are on display there.

After about a whole year, Bayar's parents let her move in with me when she turned eighteen on August 7, 2004. Her parents moved five blocks away. When asked why by Bayar and I. Her mother said, "It's because Bayar and you are women now; and you're going to have your own lives with each other." Kilan told Bayar that she would still be able to help us if we needed anything, but to also have independence.

September 8, 2004, is when Bayar moved in with me for good, my apartment was also Bayar's apartment now.

APARTMENT LOVE
9/8/2004

On a Monday afternoon, I came home from the pharmacy to find four boxes in the center of the floor. I ignored them because I knew they were Bayar's. Then she came in with a small fake Orchid plant; she placed it in the extra window of the bedroom. Then she took out her book collection. A Chinese language book, a cooking book, and a Chinese women studies in English text. I had also found amazingly Bayar loved Audre Lorde's books as well. She had two, one called *ZAMI A NEW SPELLING OF MY NAME*, and the other *SISTER OUTSIDER*. I had *THE LAND WERE OTHER PEOPLE LIVE* and poems of her first book, *THE FIRST CITIES*. And I had just got *WARRIOR POET* from Owen. In the book *CABLES OF RAGE*. Audre has a lesbian poem called *MARTHA* and I later discovered that the poem is about her.

Bayar comes back with her swivel chair with prints of different flowers on it that goes against the tannest of the chair. Then she called me and asked, "Feel, why tomorrow? How about today so we can get shopping over with." She means

The Rhythm of Poetry
Zaire Hodges

shopping for things to make the apartment nicer.

Bayar and I got in a light orange oval car with one window in the back and two in the front. We headed to IKEA and came back with colorful decorated pillows to put on the leather sofa and a desk on wheels for Bayar to write. I had read most of the time, and barely written unless I had to. But Bayar could go at it for days; just type and type lots of essays she thought about. Also I had written a whole journal of them and portions about me, Bayar, and New York.

Bayar didn't get a job yet, she said it was because she was waiting to go and be working for the children's book company writing stories. Like Eric Carl's books. The two famous ones are *BROWN BARE BROWN BARE WHAT DO YOU SEE* and *THE HUNGRY CATAPILLAR*.

So I waited a month and on December 9, 2004; Bayar got the job. She was so happy, and I was also happy for her. She was now working on a children's book of all ethnic cities; it was called *CULTURES*. She was almost done after a month working on it.

The Rhythm of Poetry

Zaire Hodges

SUCCESS FOR BAYAR

9/16/2004

After the typing was done, Bayar hand delivered it to the company she worked for and they fell in absolute bliss with the book. It was translated into Chinese, French, Arabic, Indian, Yiddish, Spanish, Japanese, Eskimo, African, Asian, Aleut, and Roman.

Stewart Martin (the children's book marketing agent) said, "Mrs. Bayar Ena's book Culture is the most popular since the African folktale book *ANOCIE THE SPITER*." Everyone and I were so happy for Bayar; everybody came over to our apartment. Cameron and Numbi, Rain and Nia; they were happy for the both of them.

Rain who was twenty one announced that Nia who was twenty-three was pregnant. Rain was three years older than Bayar and me. We all clapped when she shared the news. They said they did want baby gifts to be given by their friends but not a baby shower because Nia's mother did not approve of the baby which Nia created with her old boyfriend Eric. They were only friends now. Her mother called Nia all these nasty names, including home wrecker. But Eric's wife said it was okay for Nia to create a baby with Eric. Adding she was not a home wrecker. We all said, "Wow." when Nia finished. Then she changed the subject to craving tuna and crackers.

I went into the kitchen to get them. Bayar was in there and she asked, "Isn't it sweet that Nia's pregnant?" "Ya." I said. Then out of know where Bayar said, "I want to get pregnant at a certain time." I said, "Okay." Bayar asked, "Is that yes?" "Yes." I said. Bayar jumped up and down, and then we both laughed and went out of the kitchen. Bayar said, "I know someone else who will get pregnant, myself." We clapped and then Nia said, "Bayar next three years from now. You will have a beach ball under your shirt you call a human." We cheered towards the end of the celebration for the four-month arrival. Since Nia was five months and the three years one coming. We were all very happy.

The Rhythm of Poetry
Zaire Hodges

NEW LIFE
10/7/2005

On October 7, 2005, everyone came together to see the birth of Nia's baby. Rain, Eric, Cameron, Numbi, Bayar, and I. Nia's baby was mixed because Eric was black the baby was light skinned; she looked just like her mother. Nia named the baby Hope Ciena Meredith after Nia and Rain's last names after marriage.

The baby was beautiful but Nia began to cry when asked why she had said I am happy to give new life, but I wish my mom was with me to see Hope; she cried even harder.

Rain sat next to her hugging her and Eric rubbing her back for comfort. And the rest of us could do nothing but be saddened by Nia's disappointment about her mother. She was so hurt Rain said she cried for three days straight. And she had to get up with the baby every night and do everything. By the third day, Rain had brought the baby by our apartment and slept on our sofa while I looked after the baby.

When Rain got up from sleeping I asked her, "Do you think Nia has postpartum depression?" She said, "I don't know? I will have a counselor come to my apartment and bring Nia." Rain said she would think about it.

Rain was not tired anymore so she brought flowers for Nia. Rain called me back that same day. She said she had enough and was going to bring Nia. She said that she gave Nia the flowers and she didn't look at them. Rain told Nia she was taking her out to the mall and then drove to my apartment. Nia was asleep and woke up in the apartment in our bedroom; with me, Rain, and the counselor in front of her. "What's going on?" she asked. "Well your partner and your friend think you have postpartum depression." the counselor said. Nia said, "Well, the baby does make me tried." The counselor ran test and said, "Yes Nia does have postpartum." Rain asked, "What can I do?" He said, "Well spend time with her and reintroduce her to the baby. Also I am going to prescribe meds for two weeks and see what happens; which ones work and ones that don't."

SPENDING TIME

12/7/2007

Two weeks later Nia went to Central Park with the baby and Rain. And they looked at nature, walked around, went baby shopping, and then came home in their car.

The next day I came over while Rain was doing her writings she did from home. I said hello to her; then went to where Nia was sitting on the tan sofa breastfeeding the baby. I asked her how she was doing and she said good. I am learning the baby, and she is getting to know me. Nia said, "Thank you Felicia." I said, "You're welcome." Then I asked, "How's Bayar?" "Great, I got to get her from work; also I got to get a monitor. Why?" Nia said. "Because Bayar's pregnant." I said. Nia smiled and said, "Yes. Congratulations." "Does Honey Bee look like a beach ball?" she asked. "Ya she do." I said and Nia laughed. "How she is dealing with her belly?" she asked. "She's managing, I had to help her up yesterday. Sleeping annoys her." I said. Bayar could not sleep in the bed but on the sofa. She was asleep for two days constantly. She put the metal top and the plastic end on her belly hearing the baby placental fluid

The Rhythm of Poetry

Zaire Hodges

moving. I got to get her from work, and I left and went back to Nia and Rain's apartment. When I got home Bayar's asleep.

She took a taxi from work. Bayar called me and told me that next week she starts at N.Y.S. WRITERS INSTITUTE for her writing, and she's excited. She's just home now watching the German channel on TV; she reads and speaks German. I was shocked; I only knew French, but it's still good. One day I walked in, and she said something in German. I asked, "What did she say?" "I said love in German." Bayar said. Then she asked, "Want to watch this German tape with me?" I shook my head and walked away. Bayar comes back with a small bowl of Wheat Thins. I call her by her nickname Bay I said, "Don't you think that's too much German?" "No." she said back. "Okay." I said obeying her wish to learn more German. "I am going to get more apples." Bayar said.

Then she gets up after eating Wheat Thins and goes into the kitchen. "Eat the whole bag, it's good for you." I said. She ate only half of them; and she saved more for the morning when eating oatmeal. She ate that for two days; and then Cheerios with honey. Then one day just ate straight apples with water; and then later bread with Skippy peanut butter. I think the oddest thing she ate was a salad in the morning with everything on it; which included boiled eggs, two kinds of bacon Canadian and turkey.

On January 12, 2006, Bayar starts N.Y.S.; she doing well and enjoying it. She isn't the only pregnant one in there either. A woman who's already there, and another woman going to get a masters degree is pregnant as well. Bayar was enjoying the class. And only had two more months of being pregnant and N.Y.S. she would graduate and give birth in 2008.

INSULT TO LEAVE

6/4/2008

Nia did not want her mother to come. "She must come to see Hope." Eric said. "No." Nia said. "But..," Eric said. She interrupted him and said, "Fine but I am warning you." Then Rain agreed and said, "Yes she is something else." "Why can't she come here?" Eric asked. "You will soon see why." Rain replied.

Nia unwillingly invited her mother and she walked in quietly. Nia said to her mother, "This is my apartment." "It's quant." Nia's mother replied. "You remember Rain?" Nia asked. "Oh, yes that *thing* you fell *in love* with." she replied. Nia said, "Mother be nice to Rain, she is a human being not a thing." "Well in my book she a *thing*." her mother replied. Then Nia said, "And this is the new member of our family, our baby." "This is a family?" Nia's mother said with a sarcastic voice. "Mother pleases stop it!" Nia yelled. "Who's the father?" her mother asked. "A man name Eric." Nia replied. "Can I see him?" Nia's mother asked Nia. "Yes." Nia said. Then Nia went

The Rhythm of Poetry

Zaire Hodges

to go get him. "How is he?" Nia's mother asked. "Nice, unlike you?" Rain said.

Eric came down from upstairs, "Hi." Eric said. Nia's mother said nothing. Eric was waiting for a response and then Nia mother said, "He, He's a Nergo?" Nia replied, "Excuse me, mother apologize to our daughters father!" "No I will not! First you're with this *thing*." Nia's mother said.

Rain got up discussed. "Now you bore and conceived a child with black filth?" her mother said. Then Nia yelled, "Mother get out!! Get out our apartment now!!!" "Fine!" her mother yelled back.

Nia went towards the window and said, "And another thing you're not welcome in this apartment and you are never going to see our baby the way you behaved. Also Eric is a good guy and great father. And Rain is a better women too and a great mother."

Nia came back in and said, "You see, that's why I didn't want her to come here?" "Sorry everyone." Nia said. "You have guts to stand up to your ignorant mother to defend your home, family, partner, and child's father; that takes guts." Eric said. "Thank you." Nia said.

The Rhythm of Poetry

Zaire Hodges

LABOR OF LOVE

4/7/2008

On Friday night, Bayar had the baby at home. It came up out of the water like a new rise of a birth. Her name was Sol Ashanti Ena. The first name was Sol; Bayar picked it out, and I picked Ashanti for a middle name because it was a beautiful place in Africa that was named after the Ashanti tribe. Ena is her last name. She had both Chinese and Black features together in her.

Both Bayar's parents and my parents came. Millie and Kilan introduced themselves also Beana and Phil introduced themselves to Millie and Kilan. They all got to hold the baby. Our midwife Bea Washington wrapped Sol in a light green striped blanket and handed her to everyone one at a time. After passing her to me, they all agreed that Sol looked like a mixture of both Bayar and me. We said the next baby carrier would be me, since I was twenty-four and Bayar was twenty-three. We bought the baby back to our apartment.

(Felicia's Short Entry)

The Rhythm of Poetry

Zaire Hodges

FELICIA GETS HER BOOK PUBLISHED

I woke up out of bed, put the baby in the baby chair, and I turned the TV to Nick Jr. I was relaxing on the couch when the phone rang. I answered it and the caller said, "Hello is this Miss Felicia Enas?" "Yes it is." I answered back. The caller continued saying, "Hi I am Ken Dryer at Random House Publishing in New York. We found out about your book through your very good friend Cameron Markowitz. He said you're a great poet. I already know that he gave us a proof copy of your work and we think it's fabulous. We would love to publish you." "Thank you." I said back. Then the caller asked, "When can I meet you? As quick and fast as possible." "Okay thank you again." I replied and hung up the phone.

I sat back down on the couch and curled up in a ball from the excitement. The baby looked at me like I was crazy; I looked at her and laughed. Then I buzzed Bayar into the apartment. She came in with two bags of groceries for breakfast and she placed them down. "Guess what?" I said to her. "What?" she said back. "Random House wants to publish my poetry book." I said. "Wow!" she said back. "But I am scared."

I said. "Come, why are you scared? Look Felicia when I was scared you helped me now it's my turn to help you. You can do this." she said back and I smiled. "Go, are you nuts? Look do I have to say it in my native language Chinese? Go." Bayar said. So with that I went.

I went to Random House and I met with everyone. They were very nice people. We worked on the book for months. Then finally it was done. The title was called *My Life in Poetry*. I had a book signing, and it was funny; my pals and people I loved came too. My book landed #2 on the New York Times Bestsellers List.

CHRISTMAS GATHERING... THIS IS FAMILY

We gathered in our car and we drove to Bayar's parents' house. Both are parents were already there. We walked in we see Cameron, Numbi, Nia, Rain, the baby, my parents Pill and Beana, both Bayar, and my extended family. We all hugged and embraced each other.

Then comes the drama, they start arguing about differences between Chinese people and Black people. Stop!!! *(Bayar's mother Kilain and my mother tried to stop it, but it was no use.)* Finally, Uncle Walter blows his old referee whistle and said, "Excuse me, the two ladies have something to say." everybody paused. "You guys we would appreciate it if you would stop arguing so much, we want to have both of you be a family together without cultural differences; since we are married now." she said. "The women are right." Uncle Walter said. "For once I agree with Walter." Bayar's Uncle Jing said. "Agreed." said Mama Ramona and Bayar's head of the family Mama Shi Shi. They all said together, "Agreed." And then everyone said back, "Okay now, let's eat a passing of both cultures foods, Chinese and African American."

The Rhythm of Poetry
Zaire Hodges

The food was passed around the table. After eating we exchanged gifts, and then we sat around talking to the family. Then Mama Ramona said, "Wait!" "Wait!" Uncle Jing said to our family. Then everyone repeated him in a vibrant cheer to our family!!! And we left exhilarated.

When we got in, I put the baby to bed, and I walked in our room. "You know Uncle Jing is right." Bayar said. "This is family, think about it; we got these people together, had a wedding, and then a baby to smother in all the acceptance and warm love. This is family."

Signed Felicia Ena's Poet, Family, Wife, Human, and Mother.

ABOUT THE AUTHOR
ZIARE HODGES

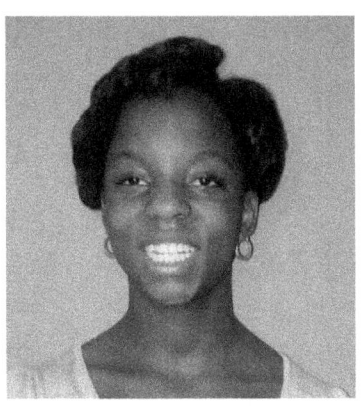

I had chosen to be an author when I was in first grade in class when we had begun free writing and I enjoyed it. Then I thought back to when I was six years old, that it's free writing so that means it's free?

I told my teacher, I wanted to write a story. She said, "Sit at the computer." I sat and ideas flowed out of me. I wrote my first story about adoption; I included photos from a magazine. When I wrote it I just thought I was writing like a typical first grader.

After I was finished, my teacher helped me read it. I was stunned at how good I was. From then on, I had written something new every week.

The Rhythm of Poetry
Zaire Hodges

When I saw my little first grade hands typing away, I loved it. My teacher adored my stories. She even went as far as laminating my stories with plastic spiral binding. I felt like a real writer.

I continued writing from first grade to the fifth. I secretly think my teacher wrote. She loves to write letters and then signs her name.

To get this point sixteen years later is amazing, and I am extremely thankful to all that got me to this dream.

Zaire

www.ingramcontent.com/pod-product-compliance
Lightning Source LLC
Chambersburg PA
CBHW071846290426
44109CB00017B/1940